© 1990 Franklin Watts

First published in the USA by
Franklin Watts Inc
387 Park Avenue South
New York
NY 10016

Library of Congress Cataloguing-in-Publication Data
Stephen, R. J.
　　Combat Aircraft, R. J. Stephen.
　　　p.　cm. — (Picture world)
　　Includes index.
　　Summary: An introduction to the various types of warplanes used by
today's air forces.
　　ISBN 0-531-14009-1
　　1. Airplanes, Military—Juvenile literature.　[1. Airplanes,
Military.]　I. Title.　II. Series.
UG1240.B37　1990　　　　　　　　　　　　　　　　　　　　　　89-38497
358.4'183—dc20　　　　　　　　　　　　　　　　　　　　　　　　　CIP
　　　　　　　　　　　　　　　　　　　　　　　　　　　　　　　　　　AC

Printed in Belgium

Series Editor
Norman Barrett

Designed by
K and Co.

Photographs by
Boeing Aerospace
Boeing Military Airplane
　Company
British Aerospace
Lockheed Aircraft Corporation
MBB
Rockwell International
Shorts
Swedish Air and Military Attaché
U.S. Navy
U.S. Navy/Lt Baranek
U.S. Navy/Lt Cmdr Leenhouts
U.S. Navy/PH2 B. R. Trombecky
Xinhua News Agency

Technical Consultant
Bernie Fitzsimons

The Picture World of

Combat Aircraft

R. J. Stephen

CONTENTS

Franklin Watts

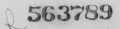

New York • London • Sydney • Toronto

Introduction

Aircraft play an important part in all branches of the armed forces. The major powers of the world have fleets of aircraft attached to their navies and armies, as well as large air forces.

Several kinds of aircraft are used for different purposes. Some are specialized, such as bombers and transports. Others can perform more than one task.

▽ A Tornado fighter fires a Sky Flash air-to-air missile.

◁ A Sea Harrier comes in to land on the deck of an aircraft carrier. Naval aircraft have several duties, including hunting submarines and protecting the fleet against attack from the air.

▽ A Soviet reconnaissance aircraft, or "snooper" (front), is intercepted by a U.S. fighter, an F-15 Eagle.

Air power

The chief purpose of a nation's forces is to deter aggression. Aircraft are part of the overall military strategy. Their job is to protect and defend over land and sea. In a state of war, they are used to attack enemy forces and military positions.

▽ Combat aircraft carry missiles and other equipment in their bomb bay, and on pylons under the fuselage and wings.

△ A Harrier sits behind an array of missiles, bombs and other weapons it is capable of carrying for its ground attack or air defense roles.

▷ A squadron of Airguard interceptor fighters of the Chinese Air Force.

9

Flying a plane is a skilled job. Only the very best pilots qualify to fly modern fighters.

Pilots of combat aircraft must be able to make split-second decisions when flying at supersonic speeds, sometimes under heavy attack from the enemy. They have a whole armory of weapons and missiles under their control.

▷ Flying is the next step in a pilot's training. These Hawk trainers have separate controls for an instructor sitting behind the pilot.

▽ The cockpit display of an aircraft simulator. This is not in a real airplane, but is a device used on the ground for training pilots. The controls and instruments are exactly as in a real cockpit. The pilot has to react to the scene projected on a screen.

▷ (Inset) Ground staff loading a missile. The duties of air force personnel on the ground include maintaining aircraft and weapons, loading bombs and missiles, and refueling aircraft.

Fighters

Fighters may be divided into two main kinds. The traditional fighter engages in close combat with enemy aircraft. Without advanced radar, it may be able to operate only during the day.

The other kind, sometimes called interceptors, are designed to attack enemy aircraft with long-range missiles.

△ F/A-18 Hornets of the U.S. Navy. The prefix F/A means the Hornet has a dual role as a fighter (F) and an attack (A) aircraft.

▷ The Tornado ADV (air defense variant) is a long-range interceptor. It carries a drop tank, holding fuel, under each wing.

△ The F-16 Fighting Falcon is a day closecombat fighter. It is armed with a cannon and wingtip missiles, and can be maneuvered readily at high speeds.

▽ This rear view of a Tornado shows its afterburners in action. These are devices that produce extra thrust by burning fuel in the exhausts of the engines.

▷ An F-4 Phantom II of the U.S. Navy in a steep climb. The Phantom is an all-purpose fighter that operates from land or ship. It was once one of the most popular fighters in the air forces of the West.

▽ Two more U.S.-built fighters, the F-5 Tiger II (front) and the F-14 Tomcat. The missile on the Tiger's wingtip is a Sidewinder.

Bombers

Specialized aircraft are used for striking deep into enemy territory. These are called strategic bombers. They approach their targets at low level and release missiles from a distance.

Some fighters are also used for bombing missions. These fighter-bombers fly in low to attack enemy targets such as supply columns or airfields.

◁ The Rockwell B-1B was designed to replace the B-52 bomber in the U.S. Air Force. It can fly at supersonic speeds, but relies on stealth to penetrate enemy defenses. Although it is the same size as the Boeing B-52, it shows up on radar screens 100 times smaller. It can deliver cruise missiles or nuclear bombs as well as short-range missiles.

△ The B-2 stealth
bomber on its first
flight, in July, 1989.
This all-wing bomber,
the most expensive
aircraft ever built, is
designed to avoid
detection by radar or
heat-seeking missiles.
It can carry 25 tons of
nuclear warheads.

▷ An F-111 fighter-
bomber drops a
cluster of bombs.

Attack aircraft

Attack aircraft are used for assault missions against enemy forces on the surface. They make raids against enemy troops on or near the battlefield.

Attack aircraft can be armed with laser-guided and cluster bombs, packs of rockets, machine-guns and cannon.

▽ Jaguars on a low-level flying exercise. The boxlike structures on either side of the fuselage are the engine air intakes.

△ This underbody view shows a Jaguar with two laser-guided bombs on its inner pylons, pods on its outer pylons with devices for jamming radar signals and confusing guided missiles, and a fuel tank in the center.

▷ An A-6 Intruder monitors the flight of two low level laser-guided bombs. The Intruder is used by the heavy attack squadrons of the U.S. Navy and Marines, and can deliver both conventional and nuclear weapons.

△ An unusual view of an A-7E Corsair pilot, with two other Corsairs of the squadron in formation behind him. Corsairs are light attack aircraft used by the U.S. Navy.

▽ An A-4 Skyhawk firing its 20mm cannon. Another light attack aircraft, the Skyhawk can also carry nuclear weapons.

▽ An AJ 37 Viggen of the Swedish Air Force takes off. An all-weather aircraft, the AJ 37 is designed for attacking surface targets on land and at sea. It has a short take-off run, like all Swedish combat aircraft, for operations from roads.

Various kinds of aircraft may be used for assault duties, from converted light transports to supersonic jets.

When nuclear weapons are used, the aircraft carrying them are sometimes called strike aircraft. They usually have more distant missions, similar to those of the heavy bomber.

Other combat aircraft

Not all military aircraft are used for fighting or bombing.

Reconnaissance and communications aircraft collect information and pass it on. Some reconnaissance aircraft fly high and fast, spying on enemy bases. Others are equipped with special radar to detect enemy aircraft or missiles.

Transport aircraft carry troops and equipment. Tankers are used for refueling aircraft in mid-air.

▽ A Boeing tanker refuels a fighter in mid-air. Variations of civil transports are built for military use as tankers and transports.

▷ The Boeing E-3 Sentry, based on the 707 airframe, is used for reconnaissance. It is, in effect, a flying radar station. It is designed to give early warning of enemy approach, and can detect aircraft and missiles at great distances.

◁ The E-6A TACAMO is also built on the 707 airframe. TACAMO stands for "TAke Charge And Move Out," and its job is to act as a link between the U.S. National Command and the Navy's ballistic missile submarines.

▷ The C-130H Hercules can carry nearly 100 troops. Hercules transports are used in more than 50 countries. They have been built for several non-transport uses, such as reconnaissance, in-flight refueling and minelaying.

Air shows

Air shows provide the public with displays of flying and show off new aircraft and ideas. The big air shows attract both civil and military aircraft from many parts of the world. They are used as a market-place for selling aircraft and arms to other countries.

Air displays include mock close-combat "dogfights," formation flying and breathtaking aerobatics.

▽ The Hawks of the famous Red Arrows perform a spectacular "bomb burst." The Red Arrows are the aerobatics display team of the Royal Air Force. They give displays all over the world.

△ Formation flying by the Red Arrows.

▷ Hornets of the Blue Angels, the flight demonstration squadron of the United States Navy, perform a "Fortus." This remarkable back-to-back maneuver calls for precision flying of great skill.

Fastest and highest

The fastest combat aircraft is a reconnaissance plane, the Blackbird, or Lockheed SR-71A. In favorable conditions, it can fly at more than three times the speed of sound, and has set a world record of 2,193 mph (3,530 km/h).

It has flown at a height of over 85,069 ft (25,929 meters), higher than any other military aircraft in service.

The Blackbird, which is not armed, was commissioned by the CIA (Central Intelligence Agency) for carrying out strategic reconnaissance missions.

Straight up and down

Some aircraft have been designed to take off and land without a runway, in the same way as a helicopter. This technique is called V/STOL, for Vertical/Short Take-Off and Landing.

The advantage of such aircraft, sometimes called jump-jets, is that they do not need long, specially prepared runways. They can operate from small airfields near the battlefield, or from small aircraft carriers or other ships with small flight decks.

The most successful jump-jet has been the Harrier, which is used by the RAF and the U.S. Marines.

△ The Blackbird, the fastest and highest-flying combat aircraft.

△ The Harrier, a jump-jet aircraft, taking off vertically.

Swing wings

Some aircraft are designed with "swing wings." This feature, also called "variable geometry," allows the position of the wings to be changed during flight. Swing-wing aircraft take off and operate at low speeds with their wings in the forward position. But for traveling at supersonic speeds, they have the wings swept back, forming a triangular shape with the tail.

Swing-wing aircraft include the Tornado and the F-111.

△ A Soviet swing-wing fighter, the MiG-23, with wings in the forward position.

Alarming missiles

ALARM stands for Air-Launched Anti-Radiation Missile. Anti-radiation missiles are programmed to zero in on enemy radar transmitters. The message intended is "Switch off, or be blown up!"

Defense against SAM

The SAM, or Surface-to-Air Missile, is a deadly enemy of combat aircraft. Much of the design, tactics and electronics of modern warplanes is devised to counter or evade attack from below.

Aircraft fly fast and low to avoid being picked up on enemy radar, and they operate systems such as ALARM to counter it. They also carry pods that dump flares or chaff to divert oncoming missiles.

△ A soldier fires a Javelin SAM from a portable launcher.

Glossary

Afterburner
A feature of certain engines that gives extra thrust by burning fuel in the exhaust section.

Air intake
The opening in a jet engine that takes in air from the outside.

Ballistic missiles
Long-range nuclear missiles.

Cruise missile
A missile equipped with a computer system that enables it to zero in on a very distant target with great accuracy, flying low to avoid enemy radar.

Interceptors
Fighters that have the task of attacking enemy aircraft at long range.

Jump-jet
A V/STOL aircraft.

Pylons
Structures under an airplane's body and wings to which missiles, weapons, extra fuel tanks and special devices may be attached.

Radar
A device for sending out special radio waves to detect motion of aircraft.

Reconnaissance aircraft
Aircraft that is often unarmed and used to seek information, particularly about enemy movements and installations.

Strike aircraft
Attack aircraft which can use conventional or nuclear weapons.

Supersonic
Faster than the speed of sound.

Swing wings
Wings whose position can be altered during flight.

V/STOL aeroplane
One that can take off and land vertically or with a short take off roll.

Index